OUR
GR★★T
STATES

WHAT'S GREAT ABOUT
NEVADA?

✴ Rebecca Felix

LERNER PUBLICATIONS ✴ MINNEAPOLIS

# CONTENTS

## NEVADA
# WELCOMES YOU! ✳ 4

Lerner Publications Company
A division of Lerner Publishing Group, Inc.
241 First Avenue North
Minneapolis, MN 55401 USA

For reading levels and more information, look
up this title at www.lernerbooks.com.

Main body text set in ITC Franklin Gothic Std
Book Condensed 12/15.
Typeface provided by Adobe Systems.

Library of Congress Cataloging-in-Publication
Data

Felix, Rebecca, 1984–
        What's great about Nevada? / by
Rebecca Felix.
            pages cm. — (Our great states)
        Includes index.
        Audience: Grades 4–6.
        ISBN 978-1-4677-3880-4 (lib. bdg. :
alk. paper) — 978-1-4677-8511-2 (pbk.) —
ISBN 978-1-4677-8512-9 (EB pdf)
        1. Nevada—Juvenile literature.
I. Title.
F841.3.F47  2016
979.3—dc23                    2015000984

Manufactured in the United States of America
1 - PC - 7/15/15

# NEVADA Welcomes You!

Welcome to Nevada! Here dusty deserts surround big cities. Bright flowers bloom on cacti. Wild horses and roadrunners roam the desert. Music, street performers, and vacationers create a buzz of activity on the streets of glittery Las Vegas. You can enjoy rodeos, concerts, and magic shows. Take a swim in the icy-blue waters of Lake Tahoe. Or zip through the desert in dune buggies and tour towering canyons of red rocks. You'll never run out of things to do in Nevada. Read on to learn about ten places that make this state great!

OREGON

IDAHO

Miles
0 20 40 60 80
0 40 80 120
Kilometers

N

GREAT

SHOSHONE MOUNTAINS

BASIN

UTAH

Reno  Sparks

**Carson City**

Lake Tahoe

Walker River

Boundary Peak
(13,140 feet/
4,005 m)

Meadow Valley Wash

Las Vegas

North Las Vegas

Lake Mead

Red Rock Canyon National Conservation Area

Spring Valley

Enterprise

Paradise

Henderson

Sunrise Manor

CALIFORNIA

ARIZONA

Colorado River

Explore Nevada's cities and all the places in between! Just turn the page to find out all about the SILVER STATE. >

# LAS VEGAS

> Have you ever skydived indoors? Or watched a volcano erupt? These adventures and more are packed into one giant city. Welcome to Las Vegas!

Las Vegas is a city world famous for its casinos. Walking the streets, you'll see fancy hotels, wacky museums, and celebrity impersonators. There are also huge replicas of New York City's Statue of Liberty and France's Eiffel Tower.

Be sure to check out Las Vegas's outdoor adventures too. The Golden Nugget Hotel has a clear waterslide tube shooting through its aquarium tank. You'll slide past sharks that are just inches away! Visit the Vertical Wind Tunnel at Vegas Indoor Skydiving. Whoooosh! A blast of air keeps you afloat. It also makes you feel as though you're free-falling from a plane.

Watch the Mirage Hotel's human-made volcano shoot flames and fake lava each night when it erupts.

## LIVING IN LAS VEGAS

More than 50 percent of Nevadans live in or near Las Vegas. People live near the city for many reasons. There are many businesses, jobs, hospitals, and schools. There are also lots of things to do! The city has tons of activities for tourists and for the people who live there. Visit restaurants, shows, arcades, concerts, and events. Fun can be found almost anywhere and at any time in this big city!

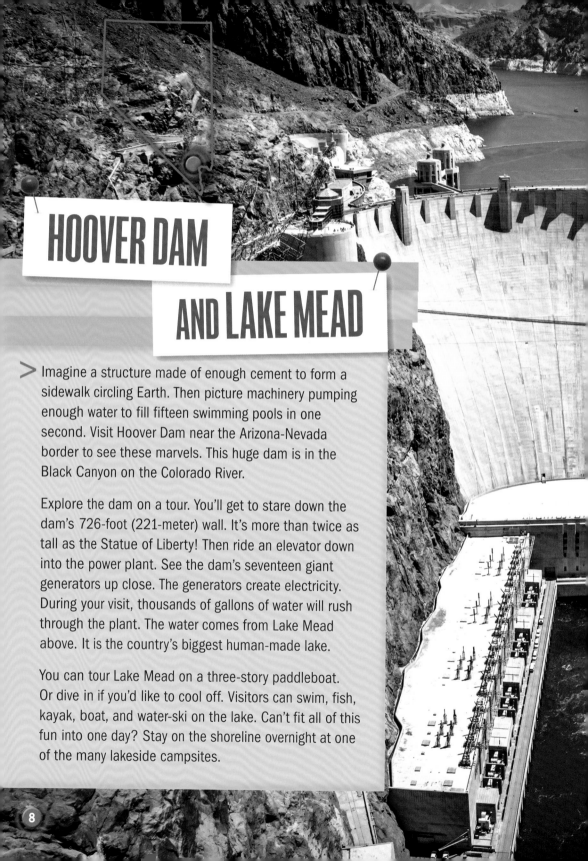

# HOOVER DAM
## AND LAKE MEAD

> Imagine a structure made of enough cement to form a sidewalk circling Earth. Then picture machinery pumping enough water to fill fifteen swimming pools in one second. Visit Hoover Dam near the Arizona-Nevada border to see these marvels. This huge dam is in the Black Canyon on the Colorado River.

Explore the dam on a tour. You'll get to stare down the dam's 726-foot (221-meter) wall. It's more than twice as tall as the Statue of Liberty! Then ride an elevator down into the power plant. See the dam's seventeen giant generators up close. The generators create electricity. During your visit, thousands of gallons of water will rush through the plant. The water comes from Lake Mead above. It is the country's biggest human-made lake.

You can tour Lake Mead on a three-story paddleboat. Or dive in if you'd like to cool off. Visitors can swim, fish, kayak, boat, and water-ski on the lake. Can't fit all of this fun into one day? Stay on the shoreline overnight at one of the many lakeside campsites.

Each generator at the Hoover Dam weighs more than four giant airplanes.

## BUILDING THE DAM AND THE LAKE

The Hoover Dam was built in the 1930s to control flooding. It holds back the flow of the Colorado River. This backup created Lake Mead. The dam is used to store water and create hydroelectric power. More than twenty-one thousand people worked for five years to build the dam. Workers coming to the area also made the population of nearby Las Vegas grow. The Hoover Dam provides much of the water and electricity to the southwestern United States.

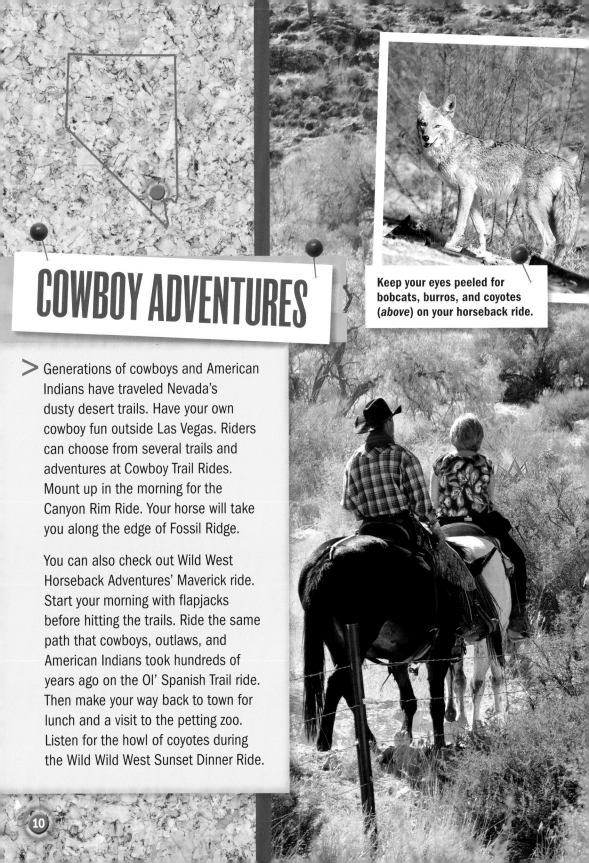

# COWBOY ADVENTURES

Keep your eyes peeled for bobcats, burros, and coyotes (*above*) on your horseback ride.

> Generations of cowboys and American Indians have traveled Nevada's dusty desert trails. Have your own cowboy fun outside Las Vegas. Riders can choose from several trails and adventures at Cowboy Trail Rides. Mount up in the morning for the Canyon Rim Ride. Your horse will take you along the edge of Fossil Ridge.

You can also check out Wild West Horseback Adventures' Maverick ride. Start your morning with flapjacks before hitting the trails. Ride the same path that cowboys, outlaws, and American Indians took hundreds of years ago on the Ol' Spanish Trail ride. Then make your way back to town for lunch and a visit to the petting zoo. Listen for the howl of coyotes during the Wild Wild West Sunset Dinner Ride.

Eat a grilled dinner outdoors and kick up your boots near a campfire after your Wild Wild West Sunset Dinner Ride.

**Look at traditional American Indian goods such as dream catchers at both festivals.**

# AMERICAN INDIAN FESTIVALS

> Continue your journey through Nevada at the Sacred Visions Powwow in Wadsworth. The Paiute American Indians hold this festival each July. Here you can see dancers compete wearing traditional outfits. Watch the huge feathers sway. And feel the deep boom of drums rattle your chest.

Sign up for the Fun Run. You'll get a free T-shirt for participating. Don't miss the special feast and the parade. End your adventure by camping overnight on the festival grounds.

Fandango is another July festival, held in Ely. The Ely Shoshone nation holds a celebration that includes a parade. Watch dancers in bright, traditional outfits perform to lively songs. Then join in the festival fun by signing up for the mud volleyball competition. Or if you need to rest, grab some traditional food and listen to Shoshone stories and songs.

## NEVADA'S AMERICAN INDIAN NATIONS

Nevada is home to the Paiute, Washoe, and Shoshone American Indian nations. These nations' histories in Nevada date back thousands of years. Ancient Nevadan American Indians lived in desert caves and mountain hills. In modern times, members of these nations live all across Nevada. The nations practice traditions and hold events to preserve their heritage.

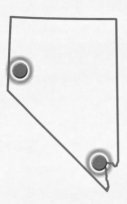

# DUNE BUGGY DESERT TOURS

> Race past canyons and up sand dunes on a desert dune buggy adventure! As many as nine people can fit into a dune buggy at Sun Buggy Fun Rentals in Las Vegas and Reno. Hop in with an adult and strap in. Harnesses keep you inside the buggies. Then hang on tight!

The Vegas Dunes Off Road Tour is thirty minutes long. You'll follow a guide over winding dune trails. If you're looking for even more adventure, sign up for the Mini Baja Chase. A professional driver races ahead of your vehicle while your driver works to keep up.

You can also sign up for the Amargosa Big Dunes Tour. Travel to the 500-foot-tall (152 m) dunes in the desert wilderness. You have four hours to explore and try to reach the top of a dune. Most people can't make it up the steep hill—will your family?

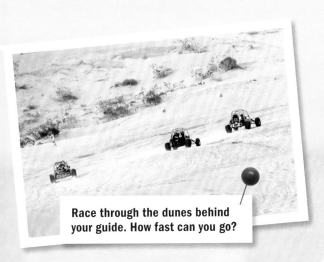

Race through the dunes behind your guide. How fast can you go?

Suit up in a helmet, goggles, and gloves before climbing into your dune buggy.

WWW.SUNBUGGY.NET
866-SBUGGIE

# VIRGINIA CITY

> In the 1800s, people dug thousands of feet underground in Virginia City. They were searching for silver and gold, and they found it! Virginia City was a mining boomtown. The town was later abandoned. You can still explore the town. Stop in at old saloons, churches, and museums. Visit a dry goods store, a fudge factory, a gold mill, and the spooky city cemetery.

Explore the rest of the city in a horse-drawn carriage or a stagecoach. Take a mine tour and visit spots where miners blasted holes in rock and hauled out gold and silver. Become a miner yourself for a day and pan for gold at the Virginia City Mining Company.

Modern events also bring big fun to this historic city. The International Camel and Ostrich Races are held yearly in Virginia City. These animals hurtle past the historic buildings on the city's main street. Enter a raffle for the chance to ride one during a race.

## GOLD AND SILVER BOOMTOWNS

In the 1840s, gold was discovered in the western United States. People moved west to dig for it, hoping to become rich. In 1859, the Comstock Lode was discovered under Virginia City. It was a huge deposit of silver. People rushed to the city, turning it into a boomtown. Western boomtowns grew quickly in population. But in the late 1800s, the US government began using less silver in its money. Silver mines and cities closed down.

OLLAR MINE

1861

Learn how to pan for gold from a miner. How much gold will you find at the Virginia City Mining Company?

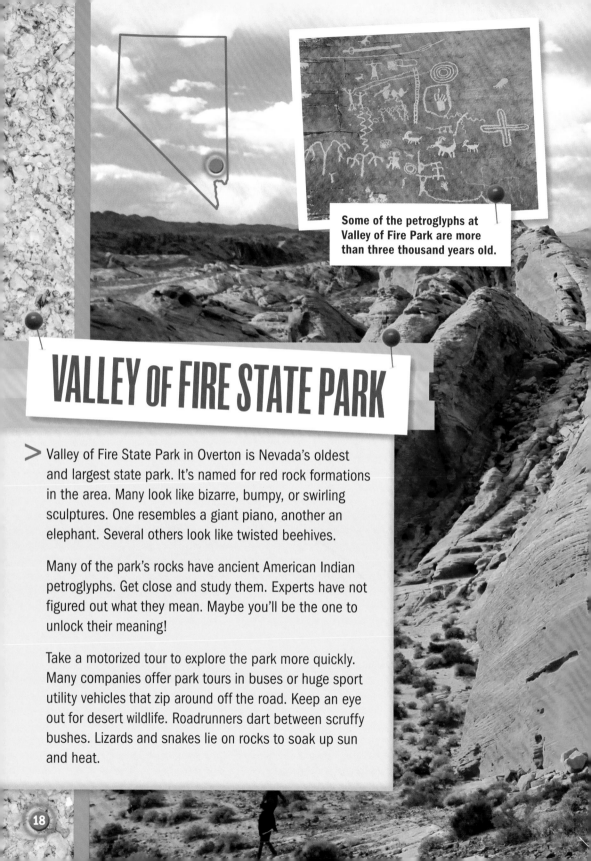

Some of the petroglyphs at Valley of Fire Park are more than three thousand years old.

# VALLEY OF FIRE STATE PARK

> Valley of Fire State Park in Overton is Nevada's oldest and largest state park. It's named for red rock formations in the area. Many look like bizarre, bumpy, or swirling sculptures. One resembles a giant piano, another an elephant. Several others look like twisted beehives.

Many of the park's rocks have ancient American Indian petroglyphs. Get close and study them. Experts have not figured out what they mean. Maybe you'll be the one to unlock their meaning!

Take a motorized tour to explore the park more quickly. Many companies offer park tours in buses or huge sport utility vehicles that zip around off the road. Keep an eye out for desert wildlife. Roadrunners dart between scruffy bushes. Lizards and snakes lie on rocks to soak up sun and heat.

## DESERT ROCKS AND WEATHER

Thousands of years ago, water passed through dunes that were turning into sandstone. The water shaped the stone. Minerals gave the rocks colors, including the red of the Valley of Fire's rocks. Some say they look as if they are on fire when the sun hits them. The area's weather can feel fiery too! The park's temperature is often more than 100°F (38°C) in the summer. There is little rain to cool things down. Nevada gets less rain than any other US state. This has an effect on which animals live in the park. Only certain animals can survive with such little water.

# BALLOON FESTIVALS

> Each September, many giant balloons float over Nevada. They're part of the Ruby Mountain Balloon Festival in Elko. It has lots of balloon-related activities. Climb aboard a balloon basket. Look up into the balloon's dome. Don't worry—you won't float away! The basket is tied to the ground. Wonder what it's like to cut loose and float in the clouds? Hot air balloon pilots are around to answer your questions.

The Great Reno Balloon Race is also in September. Its Dawn Patrol is a very early event. Balloons float toward the sun as it rises. Don't forget to attend the Pajama Party. But don't bother to comb your hair—the party includes a Bed-Head Competition!

After that, about one hundred balloons launch into the sky. You may spot mini-balloons too! Local students make small balloons out of tissue paper. They release the paper balloons in fields at the festival. Cheer them on as they float by!

At the Ruby Mountain Balloon Festival, you can catch night balloons in flight.

Once the sun is up at the Great Reno Balloon Race, T-6 jets fly in formation over the festival.

# NATIONAL FINALS RODEO

> In December, cowboys, cattle, horses, and hundreds of fans stampede into Las Vegas. They arrive for ten days of country and rodeo fun. The National Finals Rodeo is sometimes called the Super Bowl of rodeos. The nation's top steer wrestlers, bronco and bull riders, ropers, and barrel racers meet to compete. Watch riders hang on to giant bucking bulls.

Meet your favorite rodeo stars face-to-face each day at Cowboy FanFest. Some sign autographs and chat with fans. You might also run into your favorite country music singers. The American Country Awards takes place in town during the rodeo. Many country stars attend the rodeo and put on concerts.

Watch kids your age compete in sheep-riding competitions. They ride big, curly sheep! Want to learn what it takes to rope and ride? Attend Rodeo 101 clinics. Professionals demonstrate their favorite moves and answer questions from the crowd.

See how long kids can hold on to their sheep at the National Finals Rodeo.

See horses race in tight twists and circles, kicking up swirls of dust, at the National Finals Rodeo.

# LAKE TAHOE

> Lake Tahoe is a huge glittering lake on the Nevada-California border. The water is a bright, clear blue. Mountain peaks thousands of feet high surround the lake. Green pines, sandy beaches, and smooth gray rocks border its shores.

The lake and the slopes offer tons of fun activities! Sand Harbor Beach is a great swimming spot. Wade into clear water from a smooth, sandy beach. Cool off in the water and keep warm in the sun. Boats, Jet Skis, kayaks, and more are available for rent along the shore.

Onshore, explore the alpine surroundings. You can hike forest trails or rent mountain bikes and pedal along the lake edge. In winter, coast down the slopes on skis, snowboards, and snow tubes. Or cover more ground on rented snowmobiles. Zip through snowy mountain trails alongside the icy-blue lake.

## YOUR TOP TEN!

You just read about ten great things to see and do in Nevada. What would you include if you were planning a trip? Which Nevada sights would you like to see? Which activities sound most fun? Are there any places that weren't included in this book? Write down your top ten choices. You can turn your list into a book just like this one! Search online or in magazines for Nevada pictures. Cut them out or print them and add them to your book. Or draw your own!

Depending on the season, race around Lake Tahoe on Jet Skis (*top*) or speed down a nearby mountain on snow skis (*bottom*).

# NEVADA BY MAP

> MAP KEY

⭐ Capital city

⭕ City

◯ Point of interest

▲ Highest elevation

—·— State border

Visit www.lerneresource.com to learn
more about the state flag of Nevada.

OREGON

IDAHO

Miles
0   20   40   60   80

0   40   80   120
Kilometers

Ruby Mountain
Balloon Festival
(Elko)

**Great Reno
Balloon Race**

Sparks

**Sacred Visions
Powwow
(Wadsworth)**

Reno

**Virginia City**

SHOSHONE MOUNTAINS

G R E A T

N

Fandango
(Ely)

Lake
Tahoe

**Carson
City**

Walker
River

B A S I N

Boundary Peak
(13,140 feet/
4,005 m)

Meadow Valley
Wash

CALIFORNIA

**National
Finals Rodeo**

Valley of
Fire State
Park

Las
Vegas

North
Las Vegas

Lake
Mead

Red Rock Canyon
National Conservation Area

Spring Valley

Enterprise

Paradise

Henderson

Sunrise
Manor

**Hoover Dam**

UTAH

ARIZONA

Colorado River

# NEVADA FACTS

**NICKNAME:** The Silver State

**SONG:** "Home Means Nevada" by Bertha Raffetto

**MOTTO:** "All for Our Country"

**FLOWER:** common sagebrush

**TREES:** bristlecone pine and single-leaf piñon

**BIRD:** mountain bluebird

**ANIMAL:** desert bighorn sheep

**DATE AND RANK OF STATEHOOD:** October 31, 1864; the 36th state

**CAPITAL:** Carson City

**AREA:** 110,572 square miles (286,380 sq. km)

**AVERAGE JANUARY TEMPERATURE:** 30°F (–1°C)

**AVERAGE JULY TEMPERATURE:** 73°F (23°C)

**POPULATION AND RANK:** 2,790,136; 35th (2013)

**MAJOR CITIES AND POPULATIONS:** Las Vegas (603,488), Henderson (270,811), Reno (233,294), North Las Vegas (226,877), Paradise (223,167)

**NUMBER OF US CONGRESS MEMBERS:** 4 representatives, 2 senators

**NUMBER OF ELECTORAL VOTES:** 6

**NATURAL RESOURCES:** copper, gold, mercury, silver, tungsten

**AGRICULTURAL PRODUCTS:** beef cattle, sheep, hay, milk, onions, potatoes, wheat

**MANUFACTURED GOODS:** concrete, computers and electronics, food products, metal products, plastic products

**STATE HOLIDAYS AND CELEBRATIONS:** Nevada Day, Family Day

# GLOSSARY

**boomtown:** a town where business and population rise suddenly

**dune buggy:** a small off-road vehicle with very large tires, used for driving on sand

**flapjack:** a thick, sweet cake made of oatmeal and molasses or honey

**generator:** a machine that makes electricity

**hydroelectric:** using water power to produce electricity

**impersonator:** a person who pretends to be someone else

**outlaw:** a person who has broken the law and is hiding to avoid punishment

**petroglyph:** an image or words carved on rocks

**replica:** a copy or reproduction of something

**stagecoach:** a coach with four wheels, pulled by horses, that was used for transportation in the past

**steer:** an ox less than four years old

LERNER

SOURCE™

Expand learning beyond the printed book. Download free, complementary educational resources for this book from our website, www.lerneresource.com.

# FURTHER INFORMATION

**Explore the States: Nevada**
http://www.americaslibrary.gov/es/nv/es_nv_subj.html
Check out pictures, maps, photos, videos, and info about Nevada and learn about cowboys, Indians, famous buildings, and more.

Heinrichs, Ann. *Nevada*. New York: Children's Press, 2014. Learn fun facts and read interesting lists about Nevada's geography, people, and history.

Kerns, Ann. *Was There Really a Gunfight at the O.K. Corral? And Other Questions about the Wild West*. Minneapolis: Lerner Publications, 2011. Read about legends of the Wild West, including Nevada.

**Nevada Kids Page**
http://www.nevadaculture.org/indexcdbf.html?option=com_content&view
=article&id=632&Itemid=399
Watch videos, check out maps, and find exciting games about Nevada. Read about state officials, history, and more.

**State Facts for Students: Nevada**
https://www.census.gov/schools/facts/nevada.html
Read about Nevada, including how many kids live there and how many candy shops and toy stores are in the state.

Williams, Suzanne M. *Nevada*. New York: Children's Press, 2009. Read about the people and the places of Nevada, its history, and its land formations. Find state information, maps, and a timeline of Nevada's history.

# INDEX

## PHOTO ACKNOWLEDGMENTS

The images in this book are used with the permission of: © Sumiko Photo/iStock/Thinkstock, p. 1; NASA, pp. 2–3; © Laura Westlund/ Independent Picture Service, pp. 5, 27; © Chris Boswell/iStock/Thinkstock, p. 4; © Chee-Onn Leong/iStock/Thinkstock, p. 5; © Matej Hudovernik/Shutterstock images, pp. 6–7; © Jerry Sharp/Shutterstock Images, p. 7 (top); © welcomia/ Shutterstock Images, p. 7 (bottom); © Brad Boserup/iStock/Thinkstock, pp. 8–9; © Vlad G./ Shutterstock Images, p. 9 (top); Library of Congress, pp. 9 (bottom) (LC-DIG-ppmsca-17404), 13 (LC-USZ62-41448), 16–17 (LC-DIG-highsm-12017), 16 (LC-DIG-ds-04483); © Maresa Pryor/Danita Delimont Photography/Newscom, pp. 10–11; © Real Deal Photo/Shutterstock Images, p. 10; © Tero Hakala/Shutterstock Images, p. 11; © Kobby Dagan/Shutterstock Images, pp. 12–13, 23; © Mike Stotts/ZumaPress/Newscom, p. 12; © MWB/XYG/ ZOJ Wenn Photos/Newscom, pp. 14–15; © Wenn Ltd./Alamy, p. 15; © Jerzy Dabrowski/ZumaPress/ Newscom, p. 17; © Pinkcandy/Shutterstock Images, pp. 18–19; © Heather Nicaise/iStock/Thinkstock, p. 18; © nstanev/iStock/Thinkstock, p. 19; © topseller/Shutterstock Images, pp. 20–21; © Alina555/iStock/Thinkstock, p. 21 (top); © Wheeler Cowperthwaite, p. 21 (bottom); © Janet Kotwas/ZumaPress/Newscom, pp. 22–23; © H. Mark Weidman Photography/Alamy, p. 22; © George Lamson/Shutterstock Images, pp. 24–25; © Rigucci/Shutterstock Images, p. 25 (top); © Galina Barskaya/Shutterstock Images, p. 25 (bottom); © nicoolay/iStockphoto, p. 26; © Tobias Arhelger/Shutterstock Images, p. 29 (top); © 9174577312/Shutterstock Images, p. 29 (middle left); © American Spirit/Shutterstock Images, p. 29 (middle right); © D7INAMI7S/Shutterstock Images, p. 29 (bottom).

Cover: © Travel Nevada (Las Vegas Sign); © William Stevenson/SuperStock (Lake Tahoe); © Robert Alexander/Archive Photos/Getty Images (Mine); © Laura Westlund/Independent Picture Service (map); © iStockphoto.com/fpm (seal); © iStockphoto. com/vicm (pushpins); © iStockphoto.com/benz190 (cork board).